DIGITAL MARKETING FOR REALTORS

REAL STRATEGIES FROM REAL EXPERIENCES IN REAL ESTATE

DIBAKAR BALA

Dedicated to my Mother for her immense support throughout my life.

Contents

Preface

The real estate industry has been adapting to the ever-changing digital world to reach more people and more customers.

This can be both exciting and confusing at the same time, because you may not know how to implement all of these new ways of doing business effectively into your daily routine.

This book has a collection of digital marketing techniques that will help you stay on top of the latest trends while managing your real estate business more efficiently than ever before.

CHAPTER ONE

Attract customers with Geo-targeted mobile ads

Real estate is a local business, and people who are looking to buy or sell homes will turn to their smartphones as they're driving around their area.

With geo-targeted mobile ads, realtors can ensure they're reaching potential customers in real-time when they're most likely to be ready to contact a realtor.

People may not even realize that Google has an advertising tool called AdWords for Mobile Apps that lets companies create campaigns and advertise on popular apps like Yelp.

Considering how many people use these apps every day, it's a great place to look if you want your company to reach more potential clients on their smartphones.

The key is ensuring your ad stands out from others—if someone's searching for a Real Estate agent near me, make sure your company appears at the top of their list!

You might also consider using Facebook's Audience Network to target users based on their interests.

For example, you could choose to target users who have liked certain realty companies or other businesses in your industry.

You could also run targeted ads based on user location—maybe you only want to show up when people are within 10 miles of your office?

The possibilities here are endless, so it pays to think through what would work best for your brand and set up a few different campaigns with different strategies.

CHAPTER TWO

Optimize your website with keywords and calls to action

Make sure your site is set up to optimize search engine results.

SEO (search engine optimization) is an effective and low-cost way to increase visibility, attract more leads, and generate higher conversion rates.

The most effective way to do that is by targeting a wide range of relevant keywords or phrases in your website's content, metadata, titles, and image alt tags.

Aside from making sure Google crawls your pages effectively, creating easily digestible content will make it easier for users to find what they are looking for.

Remember: It's not just about getting found in searches—it's also about giving people reasons to choose you over other options.

Create a page on your site with all of your contact information, including your address, phone number(s), email address(es), and social media profiles.

Include calls to action like Contact Us or Schedule Your Free Consultation at strategic points throughout each page so visitors can quickly get in touch with you.

This can be as simple as adding links below every quote on your homepage or adding links within each section of your About Us page.

Another great idea is to add links within images on your homepage that links back to relevant sections of your website where customers can learn more about you or download free guides/brochures/resources related to their interest areas.

CHAPTER THREE

Display properties on Google Maps

Google Maps is one of, if not THE biggest search engine out there.

By including a map on your listing page you can generate more traffic and more clicks to your website.

Listing pages with maps also tend to convert better as users can quickly scan through listings via a map without having to click on each property individually.

Simply put, if you have a location-based business (i.e. real estate) Google Maps is an important tool that you need to learn how to use efficiently to maximize your exposure online!

CHAPTER FOUR

Create video content

It's no secret that video is a powerful marketing tool, but many real estate companies still aren't using it.

Don't be left behind: use video to connect with your audience and generate leads for your company.

Real estate videos are most often used for

1) Expanding reach,
2) Showing testimonials,
3) Advocating for industry issues,
4) Generating leads, and
5) Educating clients.

Video content can be created in-house or outsourced to a production agency; if you want to keep costs down, stick with in-house production.

Remember that compelling content won't succeed if you don't promote it so make sure to share your videos on all of your social channels.

CHAPTER FIVE

Create a Blog

If you want to stand out as a real estate agent in 2022, it's time to set up a branded website that you can use to build authority and trust with potential clients.

Whether you're looking to write content that is SEO-friendly or just need an easy way to publish content on social media, investing in a branded site is vital.

Not only will having your domain help establish credibility, but it can also drive traffic directly to your business if people are interested in what you have to say.

And don't let creating or updating your website deter you from sharing your expertise; there are tons of tools available that make building and managing sites simple, even if it's not something you do every day.

Get started by checking out Squarespace and Wix, two great options for anyone who doesn't know how to code.

Another great tactic for using digital marketing techniques to expand your reach is blogging.

Since 2011, blogging has grown steadily as one of the most effective ways to market online because so many people use search engines to find products and services—and according to WordStream, 84% of all B2B marketers surveyed said they consider blogs very important when it comes to influencing purchasing decisions.

What makes blogging such a valuable marketing tool?

In addition to being an excellent way to share your knowledge and connect with local customers, blogging is also a fantastic platform for generating leads.

According to HubSpot, companies that maintain active blogs generate 67% more leads per month than those without them.

More than 60% of companies cited lead generation as their main reason for starting a company blog.

By writing posts about local topics relevant to your target audience and including links back to your site (along with enticing CTAs), you can attract new visitors who may become future customers.

Plus, once you start attracting readers through regular posting, you'll be able to capture their contact information through opt-in forms at the end of each post—which means fresh leads coming into your pipeline regularly!

CHAPTER SIX

Invite guest authors to write on your blog

You can invite guest authors to write on your blog.

Ask fellow Realtors in your community to contribute a post.

You can even approach real estate agents who may have a website of their own, but no website content.

This is a great way to expand your social media presence and target more potential homebuyers and sellers.

Your guest bloggers will appreciate getting free exposure for their business as well!

Since these are contributors and not employees, they'll be happy to write an original piece just for you and link back to their business sites.

Guest blogging has gained popularity over recent years because it provides another outlet for those with something valuable to say to get that message out there.

A good place to start looking for potential guest bloggers is at industry conferences, meetups, or even within your local area network (LAN).

For example, if you're trying to find local writers in New York City, try joining Meetup groups such as NYC Tech Events or NYC Social Media Club where you might find other like-minded professionals who want some extra exposure.

Another benefit of inviting guest writers onto your site is that they often share it on their networks—something that wouldn't happen if you were simply writing all of your content yourself.

CHAPTER SEVEN

Promote your content on social media channels

The biggest mistake we see realtors make is that they stop talking to their customers once they've made a sale.

This is a big mistake because you can turn your new customers into repeat buyers by building relationships with them over time.

Social media is one of many ways to stay in touch with your clients, so don't forget to promote your content (and business) across your social media channels.

Be sure to use #hashtags and @mention key influencers on Twitter and LinkedIn. You should also be leveraging local city groups on Facebook and Instagram.

CHAPTER EIGHT

Boost business through Facebook advertising

Facebook ads are a great option for Realtors because they let you target very specific audiences based on demographic information, location, interests, and behaviors.

With Facebook ads, you can find leads for your business and get them in front of your sales team faster than ever before.

So if you haven't tried Facebook advertising yet (or have only experimented with it to date), give it another shot; these tips should help make it even more effective for your business.

The most important thing to remember about Facebook is that its users are on it all day long.

And since everyone else is doing it, that means there's no reason why you shouldn't be too!

As such, we recommend getting started by adding one or two little daily tasks into your schedule—for example: Check Facebook Ads Manager at 2 p.m., and spend 15 minutes reviewing your account settings, campaigns, and creative ideas.

After just a few days of doing that, your comfort level will increase dramatically!

CHAPTER NINE

Buy targeted Google Ads using demographics and interests

While it might sound a little scary to spend money on ads that only people interested in real estate will see, there's no arguing with the results.

When you target your ads using demographics and interests, you can significantly lower your cost per conversion while still getting higher-quality leads.

The best part?

Unlike some forms of digital marketing that can be time-consuming and hard to track, Google Ads are easy to manage and measure, so you can be sure you're making a worthwhile investment of your time and money.

After all, every dollar spent is another dollar toward achieving your goals—and if those goals include creating highly targeted prospects, advertising through Google might just be worth its weight in gold.

It's also important to note that these aren't necessarily traditional digital marketing techniques.

Traditional approaches like email campaigns or content creation may work well for other businesses, but they don't always work as well for realtors.

For example, even though many homebuyers start their search online, few look at websites or blogs before they reach out to an agent.

CHAPTER TEN

Measure success using Facebook Insights, AdWords, SEMRush, BuzzSumo, and more

Track your success by analyzing what content resonates best with your audience, which keywords you rank highest for, and which content works best in terms of getting shared.

The more insight you have into what content people want to see, the better informed your decisions will be.

Make sure you're tracking different metrics including how much time people spend on your site and where they come from.

Take it a step further by setting up goals within Google Analytics to make sure your strategies are aligned with business goals.

For example, if you've noticed that people are spending an excessive amount of time on your website, then there's likely something wrong with either their experience or search engine optimization (SEO).

If there's something wrong with SEO then try changing things like keyword density or maybe even consider relocating your page to another domain.

If users are staying on your website too long but bounce off immediately after clicking through from a search engine result, then look at ways to improve upon landing page design such as reducing friction points or creating clearer calls-to-action (CTAs).

Or, just as easily, look at optimizing user experience based upon who is coming through via organic searches and who is coming through via paid campaigns.

As a realtor, you should be looking at local data to get a feel for whether homes listed in your area are selling faster than average.

Additionally, track seasonal trends and adjust accordingly.

For example, during certain times of the year, some areas get slammed with snow while others get hit with severe storms—that can have an impact on traffic patterns throughout your region.

You may find that certain times of year work better than others when it comes to driving traffic to listings so take note of trends over time and optimize accordingly.

Conclusion

When it comes to digital marketing techniques for realtors, you have plenty of options at your disposal.

Whether you choose to build an email list or drive traffic from Google AdWords, always keep in mind that people are always searching online for homes.

That means there's a huge opportunity to get leads if you know how to leverage SEO and PPC effectively.

Focus on writing search engine optimized copy and distributing sponsored ads when running paid campaigns online – both tactics will help ensure that you attract more qualified leads down the road.

Also, don't forget about creating shareable content!

After all, what good is an awesome video or infographic if no one ever sees it? Create compelling visual assets that provide value to viewers, then promote them across social media channels like Facebook and Twitter.

Not only will these posts help you gain new followers and likes, but they'll also increase awareness of your brand as well.

Just remember: You can do everything right with your digital marketing efforts, but if you don't measure their effectiveness correctly, then it doesn't matter.

Printed by Libri Plureos GmbH in Hamburg,
Germany